GOD

A Companion for Seekers

by DAVID SCHILLER

WORKMAN PUBLISHING · NEW YORK

Library of Congress Cataloging-in Publication Data
God : a guide for seekers / [compiled] by David Schiller.
p. cm.
ISBN 0-7611-2600-7 (alk. paper)
1. God—Quotations, maxims, etc. I. Schiller, David

PN6084.R3 G59 2002
211—dc21 2002072374

Workman books are available at special discounts when purchased in bulk for
premiums and sales promotions as well as for fund-raising or educational use.
Special editions or book excerpts can also be created to specification.
For details, contact the Special Sales Director at the address below:

Workman Publishing
708 Broadway
New York, NY 10003

Printed in the U.S.

First printing
10 9 8 7 6 5 4 3 2 1

For

Clara, Theo & Quinn

With special thanks to Peter for his support,
Ruth for her guidance and wisdom, Paul and Paul for the
generosity of their talent, Bill for his inspiration,
and Barbie Altorfer, Arielle Simon, and Robyn Schwartz
for their hard work. And to Asa, as ever.

CONTENTS

INTRODUCTION · *vii*

ONE THE ATTRACTION · *1*

TWO PRAISE AND LOVE · *51*

THREE SEEKING · *85*

FOUR YEARNING · *117*

FIVE THE MERGE · *137*

SIX QUESTIONING · *169*

SEVEN SEPARATION · *219*

EIGHT WISDOM · *267*

AUTHORS · *320*

GOD is a book for believers. It is also a book for doubters. Above all, it is a book for readers who are *open,* for readers who are, consciously or not, on a path.

Not that *God* will tell you who or what God is. It will not confirm that God is the stern, gray-bearded father depicted by Michelangelo, nor will it try to convince you that God is the sound of a mockingbird at two in the morning when all your senses are heightened. But perhaps the next time you hear that bird, or recite the *Amidah,* or take communion, or push a child on a swing, you will do so with more awareness of God. Because *God* is as much about us as it is about God. It is about our relationship with this ultimate significant other—about discovery, about needs, about give and take, about perceptions and expectations.

The book is organized along the contours of a great love affair, which may on the surface sound blasphemous but which proves to be a provocative, and historically grounded, metaphor for the union of man and God. (Historically grounded: in saints' visions, in Sufi poetry, in the bridegroom imagery of the Jewish shabbos and all the religious and mystic literature that is filled with references to the Lover and the Beloved.) Like a true and meaningful love—a love where each is in the flesh and bones of the other—it begins with awareness and attraction, and moves to longing, to ecstatic union; and then to what happens after the ecstasy: doubts, often followed by feelings of separation and alienation. But finally, like all enduring love, it comes out the other side, to wisdom.

One way to think of the book is as a big, joyful discussion where no one is afraid to say what he or she thinks, and where the people talking are among our most eloquent, subtle, and impassioned writers, mystics, poets, philosophers, artists, scientists, and saints. From them come moments of discovery, moments of the dark night of the soul, moments of funny, irreverent questioning, and moments of transformation. And those ever-recurring epiphanies revealing our connectedness to Something Greater.

Another way to think of the book is as a marker on the path—or perhaps a whole selection of markers—to inspire the reader while undertaking his or her own spiritual journey. If nothing else, the book should encourage readers to ask themselves the big questions about God. It did so for me. As one who grew up in a secular household, God meant religion, and religion was what other people's families did on Sunday morning. God had nothing to do with our Christmas tree—or, on my father's side of the family, the annual Passover dinner. Until one day my friends and I, then teenagers, discovered a primitive Zen Buddhist center nestled among the woods and farms in the Pennsylvania hills. There, people were dedicating themselves to spiritual fulfillment in a serious yet unexpected way. There they sat in meditation, practiced calligraphy, gardened. Over the years I've returned a dozen times looking for that spot but never found it again; never even found a mention of it in all the research I did for my first book, *The Little Zen Companion.* But it started the questioning, the seeking, the awareness, and the conviction that God is right in front of us—everywhere. But it is not always easy to see what is right in front of us. First we have to wake up.

In the end, *God* is a book that can truly be taken at face value: as a little book about a big subject. A "varieties of religious experience" writ small. A personal look at the universal. A nudge to wake up. Read it straight through, or in bits and pieces. And hopefully there will be at least one moment to make you pause, and *feel* it—that transcendent something that's been connecting us, guiding us, and defining us for as long as we've been looking up as well as out.

ONE

THE ATTRACTION

Blowing through heaven and earth,
and in our hearts and the heart of every
living thing, is a gigantic breath—
a great Cry—which we call God.

—NIKOS KAZANTZAKIS

I AM THAT I AM.

EXODUS 3:14

In the beginning was God,
    Today is God.
    Tomorrow will be God.
Who can make an image of God?
He has no body.
He is as a word
    which comes out of your mouth.
That word! It is no more,
It is past, and still it lives!
So is God.

PYGMY CREATION MYTH

In the beginning God created the heaven and the earth. And the earth was without form, and void; and darkness was upon the face of the deep. And the Spirit of God moved upon the face of the waters. And God said, Let there be light: and there was light. And God saw the light, that it was good: and God divided the light from the darkness.

GENESIS 1:1–4

I've figured out what God is. He is an imaginary friend for grown-ups.

LILY ROTHMAN (age five)

God is really another artist. He invented the giraffe, the elephant, and the cat. He has no real style. He just goes on trying other things.

Pablo Picasso

Do you know that in the Hebrew Bible there isn't a single mention of God as he, or she, or it truly is? There is only the mention of the creator God who is constantly trying out new plans and failing. He creates the world and fails. He creates Adam and Eve and fails. He creates the Garden of Eden and that doesn't work. He creates a human species and fails, so he brings the flood. He saves a human being whose first act is to get drunk. He chooses a people with whom He constantly quarrels. That's the creator God.

CHAIM POTOK

I t is the creative potential itself in human beings that is the image of God.

MARY DALY

God has a brown voice,
as soft and full as beer.

ANNE SEXTON

What is God? Unknown, yet
The face of the sky is filled
With his features.

FRIEDRICH HÖLDERLIN

God is the being . . .
that may properly
only be addressed,
not expressed.

MARTIN BUBER

The biochemist J.B.S. Haldane was engaged in discussion with an eminent theologian. "What inference," asked the latter, "might one draw about the nature of God from a study of his works?" Haldane replied, "An inordinate fondness for beetles."

CLIFTON FADIMAN

Beauty, real beauty, is something very grave. If there is a God, He must be partly that.

JEAN ANOUILH

God is not a cosmic bell-boy for whom we can press a button to get things.

Harry Emerson Fosdick

God is a scientist, not a magician.

ALBERT EINSTEIN

It could not be a wall; but there could be a thin thin line there all round everything. It was very big to think about everything and everywhere. Only God could do that. He tried to think what a big thought that must be; but he could only think of God. God was God's name just as his name was Stephen. Dieu was the French for God and that was God's name too; and when anyone prayed to God and said Dieu then God knew at once that it was a French person that was praying. But, though there were different names for God in all the different languages in the world and God understood what all the people who prayed said in their different languages, still God remained always the same God and God's real name was God.

JAMES JOYCE

God is a verb.

BUCKMINSTER FULLER

I believe in God, only I spell it Nature.

FRANK LLOYD WRIGHT

Nature is the living, visible garment of God.

GOETHE

Some people think that God is in the details, but I have come to believe that God is in the bathroom.

ANNE LAMOTT

Good made man because he loves stories.

YIDDISH SAYING

Our God is a consuming fire.

HEBREWS 12:29

The Ethiopians say that their gods are snub-nosed and black, the Thracians that theirs have light blue eyes and red hair.

XENOPHANES

In the beginning was only Being.
One without a second.
Out of himself he brought forth
    the cosmos
And entered into everything in it.
There is nothing that does not come
    from him.
Of everything he is the inmost Self.
He is the truth; he is the Self supreme.

THE UPANISHADS

I have never understood why it should be considered derogatory to the Creator to suppose that He has a sense of humour.

DEAN W. R. INGE

He who knows about depth knows about God.

PAUL TILLICH

But if the great sun move not of himself; but is as an errand-boy in heaven; nor one single star can revolve, but by some invisible power; how then can this one small heart beat; this one small brain think thoughts; unless God does that beating, does that thinking, does that living, and not I. By heaven, man, we are turned round and round in this world, like yonder windless, and Fate is the handspike.

HERMAN MELVILLE

I declare with perfect faith
that prayer preceded God.
Prayer created God,
God created human beings,
human beings create prayers
that create the God that creates
    human beings.

YEHUDA AMICHAI

God is not a word but a name. It can be uttered only in astonishment.

ABRAHAM JOSHUA HESCHEL

God is older than the
  sun and moon
And the eye cannot
  behold him
Nor voice describe him.

D. H. LAWRENCE

God and nature do nothing uselessly.

ARISTOTLE

A little Madness in the Spring—
Is wholesome even for the King—
But God be with the Clown.

EMILY DICKINSON

I cannot conceive of a God who rewards and punishes his creatures, or has a will of the kind that we experience in ourselves.

ALBERT EINSTEIN

If triangles had a god it would have three sides.

CHARLES, BARON DE MONTESQUIEU

The nature of God
is a circle of which the
centre is everywhere
and the circumference
is nowhere.

EMPEDOCLES

God is Love—I dare say. But what a mischievous devil love is.

SAMUEL BUTLER

I affirm that God does suffer as he participates in the ongoing life of the society of being. His sharing in the world's suffering is the supreme instance of knowing, accepting, and transforming in love the suffering which arises in the world. I am affirming the divine sensitivity. Without it, I can make no sense of the being of God.

ALFRED NORTH WHITEHEAD

God moves in a mysterious way.

WILLIAM COWPER

To men, some things are good and some are bad. But to God, all things are good and beautiful and just.

HERACLITUS

Man is born broken. He lives by mending. The grace of God is glue.

Eugene O'Neill

The ways of the Creator are not our ways, Mr. Deasy said. All human history moves towards one great goal, the manifestation of God.

Stephen jerked his thumb toward the window, saying:

—That is God.

Hooray! Ay! Whrrwhee!

—What? Mr. Deasy asked.

—A shout in the street, Stephen answered, shrugging his shoulders.

JAMES JOYCE

God appears and God is light
To those poor souls who dwell
    in night;
But does a human form display
To those who dwell in realms
    of day.

WILLIAM BLAKE

There's something about music that is so penetrating that your soul gets the message. No matter what trouble comes to a person, music can help him face it. Some who didn't believe in God have found him through music.

MAHALIA JACKSON

Man is certainly stark mad; he cannot make a worm, and yet he will be making gods by the dozens.

MICHEL DE MONTAIGNE

They say that God is everywhere, and yet we always think of Him as somewhat of a recluse.

EMILY DICKINSON

I have a heavenly vase full of autumn leaves today. They look so beautiful. How much closer to God can one get?

LOTTE LENYA

Every day people are leaving the church and coming back to God.

LENNY BRUCE

God is not mocked. He is not fooled. He is not sorrowful. He is not disappointed. He is not expectant. He is not worried. He doesn't hold His breath. He does not hope or wish upon a star. He is not waiting till next year or contemplating changes in the lineup. He is not on the edge of His seat. He is complete as a spider or bear. As stone or bench he is complete.

It is only we who are unfinished. And God is indifferent as history. He has not abandoned a world He had never embraced or set much stock in.

Other preachers tell you to welcome God into your hearts as if He were some new kid in

the neighborhood or a fourth for Bridge.
What good is such advice? He will not come.
He is complete. He has better things to do
with his time. He doesn't go out. He stays
home nights. His home is Heaven. Death is
His neighborhood. Life is yours.

He asks nothing of us, beloved. Not our
lives, not our hearts. He would not know what
to do with such gifts. He would be embarrassed
by them. He does not write Thank You notes.
He is not polite or conventional. He has no
thought for the thought that counts.

STANLEY ELKIN

I cannot walk an inch
without trying to walk to God.
I cannot move a finger
without trying to touch God.
Perhaps it is this way:
He is in the graves of the horses.
He is in the swarm, the frenzy of the bees.
He is in the tailor mending my pantsuit.
He is in Boston, raised up by skyscrapers.
He is in the bird, that shameless flyer.
He is in the potter who makes clay into a kiss.

ANNE SEXTON

TWO

PRAISE AND LOVE

He is the core of the heart of love,
and He, beyond labouring seas,
our ultimate shore.

—EDITH SITWELL

Grandfather Wakan-Tanka, you are the first and always have been. Everything belongs to you. It is you who have created all things. You are one and alone.

PRAYER OF THE DAKOTA-SIOUX

I think a poet is a workman. I think Shakespeare was a workman. And God is a workman. I don't think there is anything better than being a workman.

SIR LAURENCE OLIVIER

I believe that there is such a thing as unself love and beauty. I am obliged to believe in God as a person. I don't suppose any church would accept me, but I believe in God and His grace with an absolute confidence. It is by His grace that we know beauty and love, that we have all that makes life worth living in a tough, dangerous, and unjust world. Without that belief I could not make sense of the world and I could not write. Of course, if you say I am an existentialist in the school of Kierkegaard, that is more reasonable. But existentialism without a god is nonsense— it atomizes a world which is plainly a unity. It produces merely frustration and defeat. How can one explain the existence of personal feelings, love and beauty, in nature, unless a person, God, is there? He's there as much as hydrogen gas. He is a fact of experience. And one must not run away from experience. I don't believe in miracles. I'm not talking here of faith cures—but some breach in the fundamental consistency of the world character which is absolutely impossible. I mean absolutely. God is a character, a real and consistent being, or He is nothing. If God did a miracle he would deny His own nature and the universe would simply blow up.

JOYCE CARY

Unnameable God, you are fathomless;
    I praise you with endless awe.
You are wrapped in light like a cloak;
    you stretch out the sky like a curtain.
You make the clouds your chariot;
    you walk on the wings of the wind.

PSALM 104,
translated by Stephen Mitchell

The idea of God and the sense of His presence intensify all noble feeling and encourage all noble effort, pour new life into our languid love, and give firmness to our vacillating purpose.

GEORGE ELIOT

. . . And gladly regarded the ever-changing, eternally great, unfathomable, and infinite life around him. And the closer he looked the more tranquil and happy he became. That dreadful question, "What for?" which had formerly destroyed all his mental edifices, no longer existed for him. To that question, "What for?" a simple answer was now always ready in his soul: "Because there is a God, that God without whose will not one hair falls from a man's head."

LEO TOLSTOY

Wouldest thou wit thy Lord's meaning in this thing? Wit it well: Love was his meaning. Who shewed it thee? Love. What shewed He thee? Love. Wherefore shewed it He? for Love . . . Thus was I learned that Love is our Lord's meaning.

JULIAN OF NORWICH

The pride of the peacock is the glory of God.
The lust of the goat is the bounty of God.
The wrath of the lion is the wisdom of God.
The nakedness of woman is the work of God.

WILLIAM BLAKE

God alone, in the precise sense of the word, celebrates holidays. He alone rejoices, he alone feels delight, he alone is happy, he alone enjoys absolute peace; he has no grief or fear, is free of any evil or pain, and lives in eternal bliss. His nature is absolutely perfect, or rather, God is the height, the goal, and the limit of happiness. There is nothing outside himself that he needs, but he has given a share of his own beauty to all particular beings, from the fountain of beauty: himself. For all the beautiful things in the world would never have been what they are if they hadn't been molded after the archetype of true beauty, the Uncreated, the Blessed, the Imperishable.

PHILO

Imagination is the voice
of daring. If there is anything
Godlike about God it is that
He dared to imagine everything.

HENRY MILLER

Like oil in sesame seeds, like butter
In cream, like water in springs, like fire
In a firestick, so dwells the Lord of Love,
The Self, in the very depths
of consciousness.

THE UPANISHADS

Wherever I go—only Thou!
Wherever I stand—only Thou!
Just Thou; again Thou!
    always Thou!
When things are bad—Thou!
    Thou! Thou!

HASIDIC SONG

A spirit, a fire, an essence and a light; and yet again He is none of these things.

ANGELUS SILESIUS

"What," it will be Question'd, "When the Sun rises, do you not see a round disk of fire somewhat like a Guinea?"

"O no, no, I see an Innumerable company of the Heavenly host crying, 'Holy, Holy, Holy is the Lord God Almighty.'"

WILLIAM BLAKE

PIED BEAUTY

Glory be to God for dappled things—
    For skies of couple-colour as a brinded cow;
        For rose-moles all in stipple upon trout that swim;
Fresh-firecoal chestnut-falls; finches' wings;
Landscape plotted and pieced—fold, fallow, and plough;
        And áll trádes, their gear and tackle and trim.

All things counter, original, spáre, strange;
    Whatever is fickle, frecklèd (who knows how?)
        With swíft, slów; sweet, sóur; adázzle, dim;
He fathers-forth whose beauty is pást change:
                    Praíse hím.

GERARD MANLEY HOPKINS

Hallowed be Thy name—Halleluiah!—
Infinite Ideality
Immeasurable Reality!
Infinite Personality!
Hallowed be Thy name—Halleluiah!

We feel we are nothing—
    for all is Thou and in Thee;
We feel we are something—
    that also has come from Thee;
We know we are nothing—
    but Thou wilt help us to be.
Hallowed be Thy name—Halleluiah!

ALFRED, LORD TENNYSON

God is the Thou which by its very nature cannot become it.

MARTIN BUBER

Master of beauty, craftsman of
    the snowflake,
inimitable contriver,
endower of Earth so gorgeous &
    different from the boring Moon.
thank you . . .

JOHN BERRYMAN

"You know, dear boy," Ivan said, "there was an old sinner in the eighteenth century who declared that, if there were no God, he would have to be invented. *S'il n'existait pas Dieu, il faudrait l'inventer.* And man has actually invented God. And what's strange, what would be marvellous, is not that God should really exist; the marvel is that such an idea, the idea of the necessity of God, could enter the head of such a savage, vicious beast as man. So holy it is, so touching, so wise and so great a credit it does to man."

FYODOR DOSTOYEVSKY

This is the sum and
    substance of it all—
God is,
God loveth thee,
God beareth all thy care.

TUKARAM

Our God, our help in ages past,
Our hope for years to come,
Our shelter from the stormy blast,
And our eternal home.

ISAAC WATTS

From thee, great God,
　　we spring, to thee we tend,
Path, motive, guide, original,
　　and end.

Samuel Johnson

What is the fitting love of God? It should
be as if he were lovesick, unable to get the
woman he loves out of his mind, pining for
her constantly when he is at rest and in motion,
when he eats and drinks. Even more than this
should be the love of God in the heart of those
who love him and yearn constantly for him,
as he commanded us: "With all your heart and
with all your soul."

MAIMONIDES

O burning mountain, O chosen sun.

O perfect moon, O fathomless well,

O unattainable height,
    O clearness beyond measure,

O wisdom without end,
    O mercy without limit,

O strength beyond resistance,
    O crown of all majesty,

The humblest you created sings your praise.

MECHTILD OF MAGDEBURG

I find you, Lord, in all Things and in all my fellow creatures, pulsing with your life; as a tiny seed you sleep in what is small and in the vast you vastly yield yourself.

RAINER MARIA RILKE

The world is charged with the grandeur of God.

GERARD MANLEY HOPKINS

Sure, Lord, there is enough
   in thee to dry
Oceans of ink; for as the deluge did
Cover the earth, so doth thy majesty.
Each cloud distils thy praise,
   and doth forbid
Poets to turn it to another use.

GEORGE HERBERT

God! sing, ye meadow-streams,
    with gladsome voice!
Ye pine groves, with your soft
    and soul-like sounds!
And they too have a voice,
    yon piles of snow.
And in their perilous fall
    shall thunder God!

SAMUEL TAYLOR COLERIDGE

And Jesus said unto him, Why callest thou me Good? none is good, save one, that is, God.

LUKE 18:19

We say God and the
    imagination are one . . .
How high that highest candle
    lights the dark.

WALLACE STEVENS

The second requirement in decoration, is that it should show we like the right thing. And the right thing to be liked is God's work, which He made for our delight and contentment in this world. And all noble ornamentation is the expression of man's delight in God's work.

JOHN RUSKIN

There is a silence in the beauty of the universe which is like a noise when compared with the silence of God.

SIMONE WEIL

THREE

SEEKING

God can never be found
by seeking, yet only seekers
find Him.

—ABU-YAZID AL-BISTAMI

And He is with you
with you in your search
when you seek Him look
    for Him in your looking
closer to you than yourself
    to yourself . . .

JALAL AD-DIN RUMI

Solitude begins with a time and place for God, and God alone.

HENRI J. M. NOUWEN

In every place where you find the imprint of man's feet there am I.

THE TALMUD

Lord, where shall I find You? Your
place is lofty and secret. And where
shall I not find you? The whole earth is
full of Your glory!

. . .

I have sought to come near You, I have
called to You with all my heart; and
when I went out towards You, I found
You coming towards me. . . .

JUDAH HALEVI

His name is the boat and he, my Guru,
is the boatman.
I am with him, and he is rowing,
he is rowing me across.

Mirabai

For in my nature I quested
    for beauty, but God,
God hath sent me to sea
    for pearls.

CHRISTOPHER SMART

God enters by a private door into every individual.

RALPH WALDO EMERSON

When God is silent, man must speak in His place. When God is hiding His compassion, man must reveal His love in this name.

ABRAHAM JOSHUA HESCHEL

I myself believe that the evidence for God lies primarily in inner personal experiences.

WILLIAM JAMES

If you don't make yourself equal to God, you can't perceive God; for like is known by like. Leap free of everything that is physical, and grow as vast as that immeasurable vastness; step beyond all time and become eternal; then you will perceive God.

THE HERMETIC WRITINGS

The place where
you are right now,
God circled on a map
for you.

HAFIZ

The Look of Thee,
     what is it like?
Hast thou a hand or foot,
Or mansion of Identity,
And what is thy Pursuit?

EMILY DICKINSON

The Lord travels in all directions at once.
The Lord arrives from all directions
    at once.
Wherever we are, we find that
    He has just departed.
Wherever we go, we find that
    He has just arrived before us.

THOMAS MERTON

And if you would know God, be not therefore a solver of riddles.

Rather, look about you and you shall see Him playing with your children.

And look into space; you shall see Him walking in the cloud, outstretching His arms in the lightning and descending in rain.

You shall see Him smiling in flowers, then rising and waving His hands in trees.

KAHLIL GIBRAN

God cannot be grasped by the mind. If he could be grasped he would not be God.

EVAGRIUS OF PONTUS

God, whom we see not, is:
   and God, who is not, we see:
Fiddle, we know, is diddle:
   and diddle, we take it, is dee.

ALGERNON CHARLES SWINBURNE

We need to find God, and he can't be found in noise and restlessness. God is the friend of silence. See how nature— trees, flowers, grass—grows in silence; see the stars, the moon, and the sun, see how they move in silence. We need silence to be able to touch souls.

MOTHER TERESA

We have but little knowledge of God. . . . We are like bats who cannot look upon the light of the sun. God is infinite, immense, uncircumscribed, but our intellect is finite, limited, imprisoned in this body of darkness, stained with primal sin.

CATERINA CIBO

It is with God Himself as it is with a great mountain. The important thing is to come to Him not with fear, but with love.

TENZIG NORGAY

And what do I owe You, God, for my gifts:
I owe you perspiration and suffering and
all the dark night of my life:
God I owe you godliness and diligence,
God I owe you this blackest loneliness,
and terrified dreams—
but humbleness, God, I have none and
I owe it You: for I would have You
reach down a hand to me, to help me
up to You—

JACK KEROUAC

It is better to find you,
God, and leave the questions
unanswered, than to find
answers without finding you.

St. Augustine

For thirty years I sought God.
But when I looked carefully I
found that in reality God was
the seeker and I the sought.

ABU-YAZID AL-BISTAMI

You are seeking God, dear sister, and he is everywhere. Everything proclaims him to you, everything reveals him to you, everything brings him to you. He is by your side, over you, around you and in you. Here is his dwelling and yet you still seek him. Ah! You are searching for God, the idea of God in his essential being. You seek perfection and it lies in everything that happens to you—your suffering, your actions, your impulses are the mysteries under which God reveals himself to you. But he will never disclose himself in the shape of that exalted image to which you so vainly cling.

JEAN-PIERRE DE CAUSSADE

The name of the infinite and inexhaustible depth and ground of all being is *God*. That depth is what the word *God* means. And if that word has not much meaning for you, translate it, and speak of the depths in your life, of the source of your being, of your ultimate concern, of what you take seriously without reservation.

PAUL TILLICH

You should make the way of God your occupation. The way of God is to be learned as much as a trade. You learn to have faith, learn to believe. A man that has a trade is industrious to work at it and get a living. And you ought to be as industrious and as much engaged in the way of God.

MOTHER ANN LEE

If you find God, you find life: if you miss God you miss the whole point of living.

KENNETH PILLAR

The spiritual life is a long and often arduous search for what you have already found. You can seek God only when you have already found God.

HENRI J. M. NOUWEN

What is the use of working out chances? There are no chances against God.

GEORGES BERNANOS

Whoso loveth God truly must not expect to be loved by Him in return.

BARUCH SPINOZA

God has made different religions
to suit different aspirations, times, and
countries. All doctrines are only so many
paths; but a path is by no means God
Himself. Indeed, one can reach God if
one follows any of the paths with whole-
hearted devotion. One may eat a cake
with icing either straight or sidewise.
It will taste sweet either way.

RAMAKRISHNA

Your image, tormenting and elusive,
I could not touch in the mist.
"God!" I said by mistake,
never thinking to say that myself.

God's name like a gigantic bird
flew out from my breast.
Before me thick mist swarms,
behind me stands an empty cage.

OSIP MANDELSTAM

FOUR

YEARNING

Over my head
I see freedom in the air
There must be a God somewhere

—*AFRICAN-AMERICAN GOSPEL*

Something buried so deep inside her that she had forgotten it was there rose to the surface.

> *How long, O Lord, will you forget me?*
> *How long will you hide your face?*

Loneliness, the hole in the center of her being.

> *Look at me, answer me, Lord my God!*

The response came in the form of understanding, and it came all at once, as if a dam had burst in her soul. Her search for God had been like a hand trying to grasp itself. God, who is infinite, can never become present because He is never absent.

You were here all along.

MARK SALZMAN

FIRE. God of Abraham, God of Isaac, God of Jacob, not of the philosophers and scholars. Certainty. Certainty. Feeling. Joy. Peace.

BLAISE PASCAL, written on a sheet of paper and sewed into his jacket

Batter my heart, three-person'd God, for you
As yet but knock, breathe, shine, and seek to mend;
That I may rise and stand, o'erthrow me, and bend
Your force to break, blow, burn, and make me new.
I, like an usurp'd town to another due,
Labor to admit you, but oh, to no end;
Reason, your viceroy in me, me should defend,
But is captiv'd, and proves weak or untrue.
Yet dearly I love you, and would be lov'd fain,
But am betroth'd unto your enemy;
Divorce me, untie or break that knot again,
Take me to you, imprison me, for I,
Except you enthrall me, never shall be free,
Nor ever chaste, except you ravish me.

JOHN DONNE

If we discover a complete [unified] theory [of the universe], it should in time be understandable in broad principle by everyone, not just a few scientists. Then we shall all, philosophers, scientists, and just ordinary people, be able to take part in the discussion of the question of why it is that we and the universe exist. If we find the answer to that, it would be the ultimate triumph of human reason—for then we should know the mind of God.

STEPHEN HAWKING

Stay with me, God. The night is dark,
The night is cold: my little spark
Of courage dies. The night is long;
Be with me, God, and make me strong.

A SOLDIER'S PRAYER,
found in a trench in Tunisia

In the faces of men and women I see God,
    and in my own face in the glass,
I find letters from God drop't in the street,
    and every one is signed by God's name,
And I leave them where they are, for I know
    that wheresoe'er I go,
Others will punctually come for ever and ever.

WALT WHITMAN

Prayer does not change God, but it changes him who prays.

SØREN KIERKEGAARD

O how great is God's
goodness and kindness,
that He does not judge by
the words, but by the will
and desires with which they
are said!

St. Teresa of Ávila

The voice of God whispers in the heart
So softly
That the soul pauses,
Making no noise,
And strives for those melodies,
Distant, sighing, like faintest breath,
And all the being is still to hear.

STEPHEN CRANE

I'm gonna tell God
   all my troubles,
When I get home . . .
I'm gonna tell him
   the road was rocky
When I get home.

AFRICAN-AMERICAN SPIRITUAL

God is an unutterable sigh, planted in the depths of the soul.

JEAN PAUL RICHTER

An old mystic says somewhere, "God is an unutterable sigh in the innermost depths of the soul." With still greater justice, we may reverse the proposition, and say the soul is a never ending sigh after God.

THEODOR CHRISTLIEB

I love you, gentlest of ways
who ripened us as we wrestled with you.

you the great homesickness we could never shake off,
that we cannot overcome,
you the forest that always surrounded us,

you the song we sang in every silence,
you the dark net threading through us,

on the day you made us you created yourself
and we grew sturdy in your sunlight . . .

Let your hand rest on the rim of Heaven now
and mutely bear the darkness we bring over you.

RAINIER MARIA RILKE

To believe in God is to yearn for His existence and, furthermore, it is to act is if He did exist.

MIGUEL DE UNAMUNO

Wild Nights—Wild Nights!
Were I with thee
Wild nights should be
Our luxury!

Futile—the winds—
To a Heart in port—
Done with the Compass—
Done with the Chart!

Rowing in Eden—
Ah, the Sea!
Might I but moor—Tonight—
In Thee!

EMILY DICKINSON

God, I can push
 the grass apart
And lay my finger
 on Thy heart!

EDNA ST. VINCENT MILLAY

God is infinite and without end, but the soul's desire is an abyss which cannot be filled except by a Good which is infinite; and the more ardently the soul longeth after God, the more she wills to long after Him; for God is a Good without drawback, and a well of living water without bottom, and the soul is made in the image of God, and therefore it is created to know and love God.

JOHANNES TAULER

In German the word *sein* signifies both things: to be and to belong to Him.

FRANZ KAFKA

I am deeply convinced that the necessity to pray, and to pray unceasingly, is not so much based on our desire for God as on God's desire for us. It is God's passionate pursuit of us that calls us to prayer. Prayer comes from God's initiative, not ours. It might sound shocking, but it is biblical to say: God wants us more than we want God!

HENRI J. M. NOUWEN

FIVE

THE MERGE

Lord, you are my lover, My longing,
My flowing stream, My sun,
And I am your reflection.

—MECHTILD OF MAGDEBURG

For in him we live, and move, and have our being.

ACTS 17:28

God is in me
or else not at all
(does not exist).

WALLACE STEVENS

A mockingbird sang in the heat. Sister John heard the sky in its voice.

Cicadas, the rustle of eucalyptus leaves; the music of sun and shade.

Sister John opened a fresh notebook and began to write. Adoration welled up through the pain, closing the gap between loved and Beloved. The force of his presence curved eternity in on itself; it was not her love rising after all, but his love pulling her toward him. She fell upward into brilliance where all suffering was released.

In the fire of his embrace, all that was her ceased to exist. Only what was God remained.

MARK SALZMAN

Kabir says: Students, tell me, what is God? He is the breath inside the breath.

KABIR

As spectators of great accomplishments, we thrill to the transcendent moment of peak achievements . . . that rarest of occasions when we enjoy the privilege of watching a person who can do something so much better than anyone else on the planet that we have to wonder if he belongs to our universal tribe of homo sapiens. . . . Ted Williams presided as the closest surrogate for God that such activities can muster.

As he said so often, he "simply" wanted to become so good that when people saw him on the street they would turn their heads and say: "there goes the greatest hitter who ever lived." And so he is. . . . And this—may we never forget, and never cease to practice—is the true significance and essence of enthusiasm, which literally means "the intake of God." . . .

STEPHEN JAY GOULD

Live among men
as if God beheld you;
speak to God as if
men were listening.

SENECA

What if God was one of us?
Just a slob like one of us?
Just a stranger on the bus
Trying to make his way home.

JOAN OSBORNE

I saw the Lord with the eye of the Heart. I said: "Who are you." He answered: "You."

AL-HALLAJ

Compassion and gratitude come down from God, and when they are exchanged in a glance, God is present at the point where the eyes of those who give and those who receive meet.

SIMONE WEIL

Put out my eyes, and I can see you still; slam my ears to, and I can hear you yet; and without any feet can go to you; and tongueless, I can conjure you at will. Break off my arms, I shall take hold of you and grasp you with my heart as with a hand; arrest my heart, my brain will beat as true; and if you set this brain of mine afire then, on my bloodstream I will carry you.

RAINER MARIA RILKE

Can water quaff itself?
Can trees taste of the fruit
  they bear?
He who worships God must
  stand distinct from Him.

TUKARAM

Where self exists God is not. Where God exists there is no self.

THE GRANTH, Sikh spiritual teachings

Every lock has its key which fits into and opens it. But there are strong thieves who know how to open locks without keys. They break the lock. So every mystery in the world can be unriddled by the particular kind of meditation fitted to it. But God loves the thief who breaks the lock open; I mean the man who breaks his heart for God.

HASIDIC SAYING

You are the notes, and we are the flute.

We are the mountains, you are the
    sounds coming down.

We are the pawns and kings and rooks
you set out on a board: we win or
    we lose.

We are lions rolling and unrolling
    on flags.

Your invisible wind carries us through
    the world.

JALAL AD-DIN RUMI

The Lord lives among pots and pans.

TERESA OF ÁVILA

God in the depths of us receives God who comes to us; it is God contemplating God.

JAN VAN RUYSBROECK

I believe that God is in me
as the sun is in the colour and
fragrance of a flower—the light
in my darkness, the Voice in
my Silence.

HELEN KELLER

If God is everywhere, then He is in food. Therefore, the more I eat the godlier I become.

WOODY ALLEN

God became man that man might become God.

ST. IRENAEUS

I had God glued to the roof of my mouth. I could hear the master's voice, Don't let that host touch your teeth for if you bite God in two you'll roast in hell for eternity.

I tried to get God down with my tongue but the priest hissed at me, Stop that clucking and get back to your seat.

God was good. He melted and I swallowed Him and now, at last, I was a member of the True Church, an official sinner.

FRANK MCCOURT

Though he has no form
my eyes saw him,
his glory is fire in my mind
that knows
his secret inner form
invented by the soul.
What is
beyond the mind
has no boundary.
In it our senses end.
Mukta says: Words cannot hold him
yet in him all words are.

MUKTABAI

God like a kiss, God like a welcoming,
God like a hand guiding another hand
And raising it or making it descend,
God like the pulse point and its silent drumming,
And the tongue going to it, God like the humming
Of pleasure if the skin felt it as sound,
And like the joy of being and becoming.
And God the understood, the understanding,
What is not pain but names itself with weeping,
And God the rush of time and God time standing.
And God the touch body and soul believe,
And God the secret neither one is keeping.

MARK JARMAN

My God and my Lord:

Eyes are at rest, the stars are setting. Hushed
are the movements of birds in their nests, of
monsters in the sea; and You are the Just Who
knows no change; the Equity that does not
swerve, the everlasting that never passes away.
The doors of kings are locked now and guarded
by their henchmen, but your door is open to
all who call upon You. My Lord, each lover is
now alone with his beloved. And I am alone
with Thee.

RABI'A

Where and when God finds you ready, he *must* act and overflow into you, just as when the air is clear and pure, the sun must overflow into it and cannnot refrain from doing that.

MEISTER ECKHART

God's hand is in the world
like my mother's hand in the guts of
    the slaughtered chicken
on Sabbath eve.
What does God see through the window
while his hands reach into the world?
What does my mother see?

YEHUDA AMICHAI

I had a thousand questions to ask God; but when I met him they all fled and didn't seem to matter.

CHRISTOPHER MORLEY

When you offer the Great One your love,
At the first step your body is crushed.
Next be ready to offer your head as his seat.
Be ready to orbit his lamp like a moth giving
    in to the light,
To live in the deer as she runs toward the
    hunter's call,
In the partridge that swallows hot coals for love
    of the moon,
In the fish that, kept from the sea, happily dies.

MIRABAI

If thou conceivest a small minute circle, as small as a grain of mustard seed, yet the Heart of God is wholly and perfectly therein: and if thou art born in God, then there is in thyself the whole Heart of God undivided.

JACOB BOEHME

I am He whom I love, and He whom
    I love is I:
We are two spirits dwelling in one body.
If thou seest me, thou seest Him,
And if thou seest Him, thou seest
    us both.

AL-HALLAJ

Is He not closer than the vein of your neck? You need not raise your voice, for He knows the secret whisper, and what is yet more hidden. . . . He knows what is in the land and in the sea; no leaf falls but He knows it; nor is there a grain in the darkness under the earth, nor a thing, green or sere, but it is recorded.

THE KORAN

Smaller than the small
I am that still centre
within you
the needle's eye
through which all the threads
of the universe are drawn.

PAUL MURRAY

SIX

QUESTIONING

Lord, I have loved Thy cursed,
The beauty of Thy house:
Come down. Come down. Why dost
Thou hide thy face?

—*JAMES WRIGHT*

Everywhere [in the Psalms] is the exhortation to praise the Lord, and God demands praise from men. *How* are we to praise him?

C. S. Lewis

God is of no importance unless He is of supreme importance.

ABRAHAM JOSHUA HESCHEL

Polite Society believed in God so that it need not talk of him.

Jean-Paul Sartre

Picture two children playing hide-and-seek. One hides but the other does not look for him. God is hiding and man is not seeking. Imagine His distress.

BARUCH OF MEDZEBOZH

You have to give God the benefit of the doubt.

SACHA GUITRY

God is the country of the spirit, and each of us is given a little holding ground in that country; it is our duty to explore that holding, to gain certain impressions by such exploring, to stabilize as laws the most valuable of these impressions, and, as far as we can, to abide by them. It is our duty to criticize, for criticism is the personal explanation of appreciation.

DYLAN THOMAS

"You know it makes me feel rather good deciding not to be a bitch."

"Yes."

"It's sort of what we have instead of God."

"Some people have God," I said. "Quite a lot."

"He never worked very well with me."

ERNEST HEMINGWAY

If the concept of God has any validity or any use, it can only be to make us larger, freer, and more loving. If God cannot do this, then it is time we got rid of him.

JAMES BALDWIN

To be thoroughly religious, one must, I believe, be sorely disappointed. One's faith in God increases as one's faith in the world decreases; the happier the man, the further he is from God.

GEORGE JEAN NATHAN

Momma could not take the smallest achievement for granted. People whose history and future were threatened each day by extinction considered that it was only by divine intervention that they were able to live at all. I find it interesting that the meanest life, the poorest existence, is attributed to God's will, but as human beings become more affluent, as their living standard and style begin to ascend the material scale, God descends the scale of responsibility at a commensurate speed.

MAYA ANGELOU

Ruler of the Universe! I admit that I have sinned a great deal against You, but have You granted me only honey? I have forgiven You for all the suffering, the hardship and the torment, but You must also forgive me.

RABBI YOSEF OF POLNOYE

I cannot accept God as the Good-Surgeon-in-the-Sky. Whatever tumors He may be removing, He has also planted there.

ANNE ROIPHE

God throws star dust in our eyes. What is behind the stars? Nothing.

JULES RENARD

It always strikes me, and it is very peculiar, that, whenever we see the image of indescribable and unutterable desolation—of loneliness, poverty, and misery, the end and extreme of things—the thought of God comes into one's mind.

VINCENT VAN GOGH

Remember the Book of Job?

"From the Bible?"

Right. Job is a good man, but God
makes him suffer. To test his faith.

"I remember."

Takes away everything he has,
his house, his money, his family . . .

"His health."

Makes him sick.

"To test his faith."

Right. To test his faith. So, I'm wondering . . .

"What are you wondering?"

What you think about that?

Morrie coughs violently. His hands quiver as he drops them by his side.

"I think," he says, smiling, "God overdid it."

MITCH ALBOM

Indeed I know that it is so:
Man cannot win a suit against God.
If he insisted on a trial with Him,
He would not answer one charge in a thousand.
Wise of heart and mighty in power—
Who ever challenged Him and came out
    Whole?—
Him who moves mountains without their
    knowing it,
Who overturns them in His anger;
Who shakes the earth from its place,
Till its pillars quake;
Who commands the sun not to shine;

Who seals up the stars;
Who by Himself spread out the heavens,
And trod on the back of the sea;
Who made the Bear and Orion,
Pleiades, and the chambers of the south wind;
Who performs great deeds which cannot be
     fathomed,
And wondrous things without number.
He passed me by—I do not see Him.
He goes by me, but I do not perceive Him.
He snatches away—who can stop Him?
Who can say to Him, "What are You doing?"

JOB 9:2–12

I think it must be lonely to be God. Nobody loves a master.

GWENDOLYN BROOKS

Rapture, being drawn out of oneself by God, is an experience in which one learns that God is stronger.

ST. TERESA OF ÁVILA

If it turns out that there is
a God, I don't think that he's
evil. The worst you could say
about him is that basically he's
an underachiever.

WOODY ALLEN

A vengeful, pitiless, and almighty fiend.

PERCY BYSSHE SHELLEY

My great concern
is not whether God is
on our side, my great
concern is to be on
God's side.

ABRAHAM LINCOLN

God must needs laugh
outright, could such a thing be,
to see his wondrous Manikins
here below.

THOMAS CARLYLE

God depends on us.
It is through us that
God is achieved.

ANDRÉ GIDE

Save me, O God, from falling into
    the ungodly knowledge
of myself as I am without God.
Let me never know, O God
let me never know what I am or
    should be
when I have fallen out of your hands,
    the hands of the living God.

D. H. LAWRENCE

Is man one of God's blunders or is God one of man's blunders?

FRIEDRICH NIETZSCHE

Someone asked Bertrand Russell: "Lord Russell, what will you say when you die and are brought face to face with your maker?" Russell replied without hesitation, "God," I shall say, "God, why did you make the evidence for your existence so insufficient?"

The more I know of astronomy, the more I believe in God.

HEBER D. CURTIS

You can safely assume that you've created God in your own image when it turns out that God hates all the same people you do.

ANNE LAMOTT

What's going to be the end for both of us—
    God?
Are you really going to let me die like this
and really not tell me the big secret?

Must I really become dust, gray dust, and ash,
    black ash,
while the secret, which is closer than my shirt,
    than my skin,
still remains secret, though it's deeper in me
    than my own heart?

MELECH RAVITCH

Though the mills of God
    grind slowly, yet
they grind exceeding small.
Though with patience
    He stands waiting,
with exactness grinds He all.

FRIEDRICH VON LOGAU

A God all mercy, is a God unjust.

Israel Zangwill

Though a sharp sword be laid to thy throat, still pray to God for mercy.

THE TALMUD

A picket frozen on duty—
    A mother starved for her brood—
Socrates drinking the hemlock,
    And Jesus on the rood;
And millions who, humble and nameless,
    The straight, hard pathway trod—
Some call it Consecration,
    And others call it God.

WILLIAM HERBERT CARRUTH

I heard upon his dry dung heap
That man cry out who cannot sleep:
"If God is God He is not good.
If God is good He is not God."

ARCHIBALD MACLEISH

GOD, A POEM

A nasty surprise in a sandwich,
A drawing-pin caught in your sock,
The limpest of shakes from a hand which
You'd thought would be firm as a rock,

A serious mistake in a nightie,
A grave disappointment all round
Is all that you'll get from th'Almighty,
Is all that you'll get underground.

Oh he *said:* "If you lay off the crumpet
I'll see you alright in the end.
Just hang on until the last trumpet.
Have faith in me, chum—I'm your friend."

But if you remind him, he'll tell you:
"I'm sorry, I must have been pissed—
Though your name rings a sort of a bell. You
Should have guessed that I do not exist.

"I didn't exist at Creation,
I didn't exist at the Flood,
And I won't be around for Salvation
To sort out the sheep from the cud—

"Or whatever the phrase is. The fact is
In soteriological terms
I'm a crude existential malpractice
And you are a diet of worms.

"You're a nasty surprise in a sandwich.
You're a drawing-pin caught in my sock,
You're the limpest of shakes from a hand which
I'd have thought would be firm as a rock,

"You're a serious mistake in a nightie,
You're a grave disappointment all round—
That's all that you are," says th' Almighty,
"And that's all that you'll be underground."

JAMES FENTON

God is in the gap.

SIR JOHN ECCLES

If you are feeling happy, you don't have to speak about it. Happiness is its own thing and needs no words; it doesn't even need to be thought about. But the instant you start to say "I am happy," this innocence is lost. You have created a gap, however small, between yourself and the genuine feeling. So do not think that when you speak of God, you are near him. Your words have created the gap that you must cross to get back to him, and you will never cross it with your mind.

KRISHNAMURTI

I would believe only in a god who could dance.

FRIEDRICH NIETZSCHE

Let us weigh the gain and the loss, in wagering that God is. Consider these alternatives: if you win, you win all, if you lose you lose nothing. Do not hesitate, then, to wager that He is.

BLAISE PASCAL

God sets us nothing but riddles.

FYODOR DOSTOYEVSKY

God is luck: Luck is God:
   we are all bones the
   High Thrower rolled:
some are two spots,
   some double sixes.

CARL SANDBURG

That's what ails us about God. We have "believed" in him intellectually; but we have not acted as that great fact would naturally compel our acting.

There's a heap of sense in that "God is a force to give way to—God is *a thing you have to do!*"

CHARLOTTE PERKINS GILMAN

Earth's crammed with heaven,
And every common bush afire
    with God:
But only he who sees, takes off
    his shoes.

ELIZABETH BARRETT BROWNING

I never understood theologies which would absolve God of earthquakes and typhoons, of children starving. A God who is not God the Creator is not very real to me, so that, yes, it certainly is God who throws the lightning bolt.

JOHN UPDIKE

God is the thought that makes crooked all that is straight.

FRIEDRICH NIETZSCHE

Well, God's a good man.

WILLIAM SHAKESPEARE

SEVEN

SEPARATION

*I talk to God but the sky
is empty, and Orion walks by
and doesn't speak.*

—SYLVIA PLATH

I do not doubt God is good, well-meaning, kind,
And did He stoop to quibble could tell why
The little buried mole continues blind,
Why flesh that mirrors Him must some day die.
Inscrutable His ways are, and immune
To catechism by a mind too strewn
With petty cares to slightly understand
What awful brain compels His awful hand.

COUNTEE CULLEN

Who walks with Him?—
   dares to take His arm,
To clap Him on the shoulder,
   tweak His ear,
Buy Him a Coca-Cola or a beer,
Pooh-pooh His politics,
   call Him a fool?

GWENDOLYN BROOKS

For years I lifted my hands to God. "Why was I born?" I shouted. "I had one son; why did you take him from me?" I shouted and shouted but who could expect him to hear! Only once did I see the heavens open. It was at midnight, on top of the prophet Elijah's mountain. I heard a thunderous voice: "Shout yourself hoarse for all I care." Then the heavens closed again; and that was the last I ever called to God.

NIKOS KAZANTZAKIS

God has been replaced, as he has all over the West, with respectability and air conditioning.

IMAMU AMIRI BARAKA

A little science estranges men from God, much science leads them back to Him.

LOUIS PASTEUR

A God who
let us prove his
existence would
be an idol.

DIETRICH BONHOEFFER

I shall never
believe that God
plays dice with
the world.

ALBERT EINSTEIN

God does not play dice with the universe: He plays an ineffable game of His own devising, which might be compared . . . to being involved in an obscure and complex version of poker in a pitch-dark room, with blank cards, for infinite stakes, with a Dealer who won't tell you the rules, and who smiles all the time.

NEIL GAIMAN AND TERRY PRATCHETT

Now it is such a bizarrely improbable coincidence that anything so mind-bogglingly useful could have evolved purely by chance that some thinkers have chosen to see it as a final and clinching proof of the *non*existence of God. The argument goes something like this: "I refuse to prove that I exist," says God, "for proof denies faith, and without faith I am nothing."

"But," says Man, "the Babel fish is a dead giveaway, isn't it? It proves you exist, and so therefore, by your own arguments, you don't. QED."

"Oh dear," says God, "I hadn't thought of that," and promptly vanishes in a puff of logic.

DOUGLAS ADAMS

There are times when thinking of God separates us from him.

SIMONE WEIL

I don't believe
in God because
I don't believe in
Mother Goose.

CLARENCE DARROW

It may be that our role on this planet is not to worship God— but to create Him.

ARTHUR C. CLARKE

If God did not exist, it would be necessary to invent him.

VOLTAIRE

Sophia wished that Florence would not talk about the Almighty as if his real name was Godfrey, and God was just Florence's nickname for him.

NANCY MITFORD

God is the celebrity. Author of the World's Best Seller. We have made God into the biggest celebrity of all, to contain our own emptiness.

DANIEL J. BOORSTIN

May it not be that, just as we have to have faith in Him, God has to have faith in us and, considering the history of the human race so far, might it not be that "faith" is even more difficult for Him than it is for us?

FERDINAND EBNER

If you talk to God, you are praying; if God talks to you, you have schizophrenia.

THOMAS SZASZ

The God I believe in must be responsible for all the evil as well as for all the saints. He has to be a God made in our image with a night-side as well as a day-side. When you speak of the horror, Eduardo, you are speaking of the night-side of God. I believe the time will come when the night-side will wither away, like your communist state, Aquino, and we shall see only the simple daylight of the good God. You believe in evolution, Eduardo, even though sometimes whole generations of men slip backwards to the beasts. It is a long struggle and a long suffering, evolution, and I believe God is suffering the same evolution that we are, but perhaps with more pain.

GRAHAM GREENE

I believe that many souls are deluded at this point by trying to fly before God has given them wings.

ST. TERESA OF ÁVILA

God will forgive me. That's his business.

HEINRICH HEINE

If God lived on earth, people would break his windows.

YIDDISH PROVERB

Up into the sky I stare;
All the little stars I see;
And I know that God is there
O, how lonely He must be!
Me, I laugh and leap all day,
Till my head begins to nod;
He's so great, He cannot play:
I am glad I am not God.
Poor kind God upon His throne,
Up there in the sky so blue,
Always, always all alone.

ROBERT SERVICE

One time there was great piety in heaven;
The stars passed the Bible around to read.
If only I could take God's hand sometime
Or see on his finger the spinning moon.

O God, O God, how far I am from you!

ELSE LASKER-SCHÜLER

God is a concept by which we measure our pain.

JOHN LENNON

Akongo was not always as he is now. In the beginning the creator lived among men; but men were quarrelsome. One day they had a big quarrel and Akongo left them to themselves. He went and hid in the forest and nobody has seen him since. People today can't tell what he is like.

CREATION MYTH OF THE NGOMBE, CENTRAL AFRICA

God is at home.
We are in the far
country.

Meister Eckhart

Why no! I never thought other than
That God is that great absence
In our lives, the empty silence
Within, the place where we go
Seeking, not in hope to
Arrive or find. He keeps the interstices
Between stars. His are the echoes
We follow, the footprints he has just
Left. We put our hands in
His side hoping to find
It warm. We look at people
And places as though he had looked
At them, too; but miss the reflection.

R. S. THOMAS

We are all children in a vast kindergarten trying to spell the name of God with the wrong blocks.

TENNESSEE WILLIAMS

For a Jew to believe in God is good. For a Jew to protest against God is still good. But simply to ignore God—that is not good. Anger, yes. Protest, yes. Affirmation, yes. But indifference? No. You can be a Jew with God. You can be a Jew against God. But not without God.

ELIE WIESEL

I would rather believe
that God did not exist
than believe that He
was indifferent.

GEORGE SAND

It's an interesting view of atheism, as a sort of crutch for those who can't stand the reality of God.

TOM STOPPARD

At bottom God is nothing other than an exalted father.

SIGMUND FREUD

The greatest question of our time is not communism versus individualism, not Europe versus America, not even the East versus the West: it is whether man can bear to live without God.

Will Durant

God is a comedian whose audience is afraid to laugh.

H. L. MENCKEN

God: the most popular scapegoat for our sins.

MARK TWAIN

I think there are innumerable gods. What we on earth call God is a little tribal God who has made an awful mess.

WILLIAM S. BURROUGHS

Operationally, God is beginning to resemble not a ruler but the last fading smile of a cosmic Cheshire cat.

SIR JULIAN HUXLEY

God seems to have the receiver off the hook.

ARTHUR KOESTLER

God is dead. God remains dead. And we have killed him.

FREIDRICH NIETZSCHE

I have had a most shameful and distressing
interview with poor dear Tom Eliot, who may
be called dead to us all from this day forward.
He has become an Anglo-Catholic, believes
in God and immortality, and goes to church.
I was really shocked. A corpse would seem to
me more credible than he is. I mean, there's
something obscene in a living person sitting
by the fire and believing in God.

VIRGINIA WOOLF

Perhaps God is not dead. Perhaps God is Himself mad.

R. D. Laing

Man has never been the same since God died.
He has taken it very hard. Why, you'd think it
    was only yesterday,
The way he takes it.
Not that he says much, but he laughs much
    louder than he used to,
And he can't bear to be left alone even for
    a minute, and he can't
Sit still.

EDNA ST. VINCENT MILLAY

God is not dead but alive and well and working on a much less ambitious project.

GRAFFITI

If God had died in the blare of the twentieth century and in houses too new and cheap to be haunted, one must seek him in the old quiet places, where he might still live on in retirement.

WILFRID SHEED

VLADIMIR: What does he do, Mr. Godot? *(Silence.)*
    Do you hear me?
BOY: He does nothing, Sir.
    Silence . . .
VLADIMIR: *(softly).* Has he a beard, Mr. Godot?
BOY: Yes Sir.
VLADIMIR: Fair or . . . *(he hesitates)* . . . or black?
BOY: I think it's white, Sir.
    Silence.
VLADIMIR: Christ have mercy on us!
    Silence.
BOY: What am I to tell Mr. Godot, Sir?
VLADMIMIR: Tell him . . . *(he hesitates)* . . . tell him
    you saw me and that . . . *(he hesitates)* . . . that you
    saw me. *(Pause)* . . .
ESTRAGON: Was I long asleep?
VLADIMIR: I don't know.
    Silence.

ESTRAGON: Where shall we go?

VLADIMIR: Not far.

ESTRAGON: Oh yes, let's go far away from here.

VLADIMIR: We can't.

ESTRAGON: Why not?

VLADIMIR: We have to come back tomorrow.

ESTRAGON: What for?

VLADIMIR: To wait for Godot.

ESTRAGON: Ah! *(Silence.)* He didn't come?

VLADIMIR: No.

ESTRAGON: And now it's too late?

VLADIMIR: Yes, now it's night.

ESTRAGON: And if we dropped him? *(Pause.)* If we dropped him?

VLADIMIR: He'd punish us. *(Silence. He looks at the tree.)* Everything's dead but the tree.

SAMUEL BECKETT

Yu said:
The music of the earth sings through
a thousand holes.
The music of man is made on flutes
and instruments.
What makes the music of heaven?

Master Ki said:
Something is blowing on a thousand
different holes.
Some power stands behind all this and
makes the sounds die down.
What is this power?

CHANG-TZU

WISDOM

How dear, how soothing to man, arises the idea of God, peopling the lonely place, effacing the scars of our mistakes and disappointments! When we have broken our god of tradition and ceased from our god of rhetoric, then may God fire the heart with his presence.

—*RALPH WALDO EMERSON*

To believe in God for me
is to feel that there is a God,
not a dead one, or a stuffed
one, but a living one, who
with irresistible force urges
us towards more loving.

VINCENT VAN GOGH

There is in God, some say,
A deep, but dazzling
darkness

HENRY VAUGHAN

One has to be mad today to believe in God and in man— one has to be mad to believe. One has to be mad to want to remain human. Be mad, Rabbi, be mad!

ELIE WIESEL

God does not die on the day when we cease to believe in a personal deity, but we die on the day when our lives cease to be illuminated by a steady radiance, renewed daily, of a wonder, the source of which is beyond all reason.

DAG HAMMARSKJÖLD

No one has the capacity to judge God. We are drops in that limitless ocean of mercy.

GANDHI

In His will is our peace:
it is the sea into which all
currents and all streams empty
themselves, for all eternity.

DANTE

The shortest way to God is to bring comfort to the soul of your neighbor.

ABU SA'ID

God is what man finds divine in himself. God is the best way man can behave in the ordinary occasions of life, and the farthest point to which man can stretch himself.

MAX LERNER

God is what's good in me.

JOHN GUNTHER

As a butterfly lost in flowers
As a child fondling his
    mother's breast
As a bird settled on the tree
For 66 years of this world
I have played with God

JOSSHU SASAKI-ROSHI

He loseth nothing that loseth not God.

GEORGE HERBERT

The belief in God is as necessary as sex.

ISAAC BASHEVIS SINGER

The word of the Lord falls with the force of a snowflake.

REVEREND WILLIAM SLOANE COFFIN

We cannot love
God unless we love
each other.

DOROTHY DAY

It is not God who will save us, it is we who will save God— by battling, by creating, and by transmuting our matter into spirit.

NIKOS KAZANTZAKIS

Man's most precious thought is God, but God's most precious thought is man.

ABRAHAM JOSHUA HESCHEL

The Brain is just the weight of God—
For—Heft them—Pound for Pound—
And they will differ—if they do—
As Syllable from Sound—

EMILY DICKINSON

The One remains, the many change and pass;
Heaven's light forever shines, Earth's shadow fly;
Life like a dome of many-colored glass,
Stains the white radiance of Eternity,
Until Death tramples it to fragments. Die,
If thou wouldst be with that which thou
    dost seek.

PERCY BYSSHE SHELLEY

The most important thought I ever had was that of my individual responsibility to God.

DANIEL WEBSTER

He was a wise man
who originated the
idea of God.

EURIPIDES

My religion consists of a humble admiration of the illimitable superior spirit who reveals himself in the slight details we are able to perceive with our frail and feeble minds. That deeply emotional conviction of the presence of a superior reasoning power, which is revealed in the incomprehensible universe, forms my idea of God.

ALBERT EINSTEIN

Whoever does not
see God in every place
does not see God in
any place.

RABBI MENACHEM MENDEL OF KOTZK

I
t is the final proof
of God's omnipotence
that he need not exist
in order to save us.

PETER DE VRIES

God has no religion.

GANDHI

There is a sign of God on every leaf that nobody else sees in the garden.

THOMAS MERTON

The nearer the Church the further from God.

BISHOP LANCELOT ANDREWES

No leaf on the tree stirs but by God's will.

CERVANTES

We keep thinking of deity as a kind of fact, somewhere; God as a fact. God is simply our own notion of something that is symbolic of transcendence and mystery. The mystery is what's important.

JOSEPH CAMPBELL

God is . . .
the beyond in the
midst of our life.

DIETRICH BONHOEFFER

A fly, when it exists, has as much being as God.

SØREN KIERKEGAARD

Life is everything. Life is God. Everything changes and moves and that movement is God. And while there is life there is joy in consciousness of the divine. To love life is to love God.

LEO TOLSTOY

God respects me when I work, but he loves me when I sing.

RABINDRANATH TAGORE

I believe in the incomprehensibility of God.

HONORÉ DE BALZAC

I do not believe. I know.

CARL JUNG,
on whether he believed in God

God never shuts one door but He opens another.

IRISH PROVERB

When you have shut the doors and made a darkness within, remember never to say that you are alone; for you are not alone, but God is within.

EPICTETUS

No,—what is God?
The impossible, the impeachable
Unimpeachable Prezi-dent
of the Pepsodent Universe
But with no body & no brain
no business and no tie
no candle and no high
no wise and no smart guy
no nothing, no n-nothing,
no anything, no-word, yes-word,
everything, anything, God,
the guy that ain't a guy,
the thing that can't be
and can
and is
and isn't

JACK KEROUAC

The eye with which I see God is the same with which God sees me.

MEISTER ECKHART

"Where does God dwell?" Rabbi Menahem Mendel asked some visiting scholars.

They laughed at him and said, "Why, God is everywhere, of course. The whole earth is full of his glory."

The rabbi shook his head, and said: "God dwells wherever man lets him in."

HASIDIC MONDO

I am in every religion as a thread through a string of pearls.

HINDU SAYING

God is seated in the hearts of all.

BHAGAVAD GITA

If you walk toward Him, He comes to you running.

MUHAMMAD

Sometimes—there's God—so quickly!

TENNESSEE WILLIAMS

I am often nearer to God when doing the dirty dishes than when listening to Bach or Mozart.

HENRY MILLER

There are three things that only God knows: the beginning of things, the cause of things, and the end of things.

WELSH PROVERB

There is not a guarantee in the world. Oh your *needs* are guaranteed, your needs are absolutely guaranteed by the most stringent of warranties, in the plainest, truest words: knock; seek; ask. But you must read the fine print. "Not as the world giveth, give I unto you." That's the catch. . . . You see the creatures die, and you know you will die. And one day it occurs to you that you must not need life. Obviously. And then you're gone. You have finally understood that you're dealing with a maniac. . . . Divinity is not playful. The universe was not made in jest but in solemn incomprehensible earnest. By a power that is unfathomably secret, and holy, and fleet. There is nothing to be done about it, but ignore it, or see. And then you walk fearlessly.

ANNIE DILLARD

"You know what I've always thought? I've always thought a body would have to be sick and dying before they saw the Lord. And I imagined that when He came it would be like looking at the Baptist window: pretty as colored glass with the sun pouring through, such a shine you don't know it's getting dark. And it's been a comfort to think of that shine taking away all the spooky feeling. But I'll wager it never happens. I'll wager at the very end a body realizes the Lord has already shown Himself. That things as they are"—her hand circles in a gesture that gathers clouds and kites and grass and Queenie pawing earth over her bone—"just what they've always been, was seeing Him. As for me, I could leave the world with today in my eyes."

TRUMAN CAPOTE

And God created great whales.

HERMAN MELVILLE

"Ooo, unlucky devil," she shouted, "don't you know that God is found not in monasteries but in the homes of men! Wherever you find husband and wife, that's where you find God; wherever children and petty cares and cooking and arguments and reconciliations, that's where God is too. Don't listen to those eunuchs. Sour grapes! Sour grapes! The God I'm telling you about, the domestic one and not the monastic: that's the true God. He's the one you should adore. Leave the other to those lazy, sterile idiots in the desert."

NIKOS KAZANTZAKIS

I hear and behold
God in every object.

WALT WHITMAN

How marvelous the Creator is!

What is he going to make out of you next? Where is he going to send you? Will he make you into a rat's liver? Will he make you into a bug's arm?

CHUANG TZU

And after the earthquake a fire; but the Lord was not in the fire: and after the fire a still small voice.

1 KINGS 19:12

AUTHORS

ADAMS, DOUGLAS (1952–2001) English author of the cult classic *The Hitchhiker's Guide to the Galaxy* and subsequent books in the series.

AL-HALLAJ (857–922) Persian Muslim mystic and poet who studied under Sufi masters, and was later beheaded for blasphemy after having said "I am the Truth."

ALBOM, MITCH (1958–) Award-winning Detroit sports columnist and author of *Tuesdays with Morrie: An Old Man, A Young Man, and Life's Greatest Lesson.*

ALLEN, WOODY (1935–) American comedian, actor, writer, and director. Among other pertinent one-liners: "Not only is there no God, but try getting a plumber on weekends."

AMICHAI, YEHUDA (1924–2000) Leading modern Hebrew-language poet whose collections include *Now and in Other Days* and *Amen.*

ANDREWES, BISHOP LANCELOT (1555–1626) English theologian; well-reputed Anglican preacher; one of the creators of the King James version of the Bible.

ANGELOU, MAYA (1928–) American writer, performer, poet; a civil rights activist, and author of several autobiographies, including *I Know Why the Caged Bird Sings.*

ANOUILH, JEAN (1910–1987) French playwright and screenwriter.

ANSARI, 'ABD ALLAH (d. 1089) Persian Sufi writer and exegete.

ARISTOTLE (384–322 B.C.) Greek philosopher, student of Plato, tutor to Alexander the Great, and author on everything from aesthetics, science, and ethics to metaphysics and tragedy.

AUGUSTINE, ST. (354–430) Early Christian church father who embraced the church after a dissolute youth. Author of *Confessions* and *City of God.*

ÁVILA, ST. TERESA OF (1515–1582) Spanish Carmelite nun and mystic and founder of numerous convents. Author of several spiritual classics, including the *Way to Perfection* and *Exclamations of the Soul to God.*

BALDWIN, JAMES (1924–1987) American author of *Another Country* and *Go Tell It on the Mountain.*

BALZAC, HONORÉ DE (1799–1850) French writer of *La Comédie humaine*.

BARAKA, AMIRI IMAMU (LeRoi Jones) (1934–) American poet, playwright, and activist. Works include *Preface to a Twenty Volume Suicide Note* and the play *The Dutchman*.

BARUCH TUCHINER OF MEDZEBOZH (c. 1750–1810) Hasidic rabbi in the Ukraine and grandson of the Baal Shem Tov, founder of the Hasidic movement.

BECKETT, SAMUEL (1906–1989) Nobel Prize–winning Anglo-French playwright and novelist best known for *Waiting for Godot* and *Endgame*.

BERNANOS, GEORGES (1888–1948) French novelist and polemicist, author of *The Diary of a Country Priest*.

BERRYMAN, JOHN (1914–1972) American poet, scholar, celebrated teacher, and suicide. Wrote poetry intended to "terrify and comfort"; best known for *Homage to Mistress Bradstreet*.

AL-BISTAMI, ABU-YAZID (? – c. 874) Persian mystic and founder of the ecstatic school of Sufism.

BLAKE, WILLIAM (1757–1827) English poet and artist determined to follow his divine visions. His "Universal Man" incorporates God rather than paying homage to a deity distinct from humanity.

BOEHME, JACOB (1575–1624) German Christian mystic and metaphysician who believed in the necessity of God's limitation.

BONHOEFFER, DIETRICH (1906–1945) German Protestant theologian hanged by the Nazis after his plot to assassinate Hitler was discovered. His *Letters and Papers from Prison* was published posthumously.

BOORSTIN, DANIEL (1914–) American social historian who won a Pulitzer Prize for *The Americans: The Democratic Experience.*

BROOKS, GWENDOLYN (1917–2000) American poet and first African-American to win a Pulitzer Prize, for her collection *Annie Allen.*

BROWNING, ELIZABETH BARRETT (1806–1861) English poet best known for her *Sonnets to the Portuguese* and *Aurora Leigh.*

BRUCE, LENNY (1925–1966) American comedian known for his edgy routines and critique of American complacency.

BUBER, MARTIN (1878–1965) Austrian/Israeli philosopher and author; most famous religious work, *I and Thou*.

BURROUGHS, WILLIAM SEWARD (1914–1997) American experimental author of *Naked Lunch* and founding member of the Beat Generation.

BUTLER, SAMUEL (1835–1902) English novelist, essayist, and critic known for his biting satire. Though raised in a family of clergymen, Butler steered away from the clergy and Christianity in general. Works include the satire *Erewhon* and his masterpiece, the autobiographical *The Way of All Flesh*.

CAMPBELL, JOSEPH (1904–1987) American writer on mythology and comparative religion, best known for *Hero with a Thousand Faces*.

CAPOTE, TRUMAN (1924–1984) Precocious American novelist whose works include *In Cold Blood* and *Breakfast at Tiffany's*.

CARLYLE, THOMAS (1795–1881) Scottish historian who believed that history was a "divine scripture." Works include *The French Revolution* and *On Heroes, Hero-worship, and the Heroic in History.*

CARRUTH, WILLIAM HERBERT (1859–1924) American professor, editor, and poet, best known for the collection *Each in His Own Tongue.*

CARY, JOYCE (1888–1957) English writer and creator of the irrepressible Gulley Jimpson in *The Horse's Mouth.*

CAUSSADE, JEAN-PIERRE DE (1675–1751) French Jesuit priest, author of *Abandonment to Divine Providence.*

CERVANTES, MIGUEL DE (1547–1616) Spanish novelist, dramatist, and poet and author of *Don Quixote de la Mancha.*

CHRISTLIEB, THEODOR (1833–1889) Founder of the German Evangelistic Union.

CHUANG-TZU (c. 369–c. 286 B.C.) Chinese Taoist writer and hermit who posed the famous question: "Last night I dreamed I was a butterfly. How do I not know that today I am a butterfly dreaming I am a man?"

CIBO, CATERINA (16th century) Renaissance Duchess of Camerino and niece of Pope Clement VII.

CLARKE, ARTHUR C. (1917–) British science fiction writer and author of *2001: A Space Odyssey.*

COFFIN, WILLIAM SLOANE, JR. (1924–) American Protestant minister and activist who spoke out against the Vietnam War and nuclear proliferation.

COLERIDGE, SAMUEL TAYLOR (1772–1834) English poet who, in collaboration with Wordsworth on *Lyrical Ballads*, helped establish English Romanticism.

COWPER, WILLIAM (1731–1800) English poet whose letters and hymns are regarded as some of the best in English.

CRANE, STEPHEN (1871–1900) American writer best known for *The Red Badge of Courage,* but who preferred his poorly received poems, now considered pioneering examples of free verse.

CULLEN, COUNTEE (1903–1946) American writer and poet known as "the black Keats"; a significant member of the Harlem Renaissance.

CURTIS, HEBER D. (1872–1942) American astronomer; known for his work on formation of spiral nebulae.

DALY, MARY (1928–) American feminist theologian known for asking the unasked questions. Author of *Beyond God the Father.*

DANTE ALIGHIERI (1265–1321) Italian poet, moral and political philosopher famous for the *Divine Comedy.*

DARROW, CLARENCE (1857–1938) Celebrated American lawyer, the defense attorney in the Scopes "Monkey Trial."

DAY, DOROTHY (1897–1980) American political activist and founder of the Catholic Worker movement and newspaper.

DICKINSON, EMILY (1830–1886) Reclusive American lyric poet of Amherst, Massachusetts. Many of her poems (all published posthumously) were centered around the poet's lifelong argument with God.

DILLARD, ANNIE (1945–) American writer known for her meditative essays on the natural world; she won a Pulitzer Prize for *Pilgrim at Tinker Creek.*

DONNE, JOHN (1572–1631) English metaphysical poet who took orders in the Church of England and was Dean of St. Paul's Cathedral.

DOSTOYEVSKY, FYODOR (1821–1881) Russian novelist, gambler, and author of *The Brothers Karamozov* and *Crime and Punishment.*

DURANT, WILLIAM (1885–1981) American historian who, with his wife, Ariel, wrote the monumental *Story of Civilization.*

EBNER, FERDINAND (1882–1931) Austrian philosopher.

ECCLES, SIR JOHN CAREW (1903–1997) Australian neurophysiologist; won the Nobel Prize for work on nerve cells and wrote *Facing Reality: Philosophical Adventures by a Brain Scientist.*

ECKHART, MEISTER (c. 1260–c. 1328) German mystical theologian who was charged with heresy; best known for his *Book of Divine Consolation.*

EINSTEIN, ALBERT (1879–1955) Nobel Prize–winning physicist famous for his theory of relativity and the iconic equation, $E=mc^2$.

ELIOT, GEORGE (Pseudonym of Mary Ann Evans) (1819–1880) Author of *Adam Bede, The Mill on the Floss,* and *Middlemarch;* held the view that religious belief is an imaginative necessity.

ELKIN, STANLEY (1930–1995) American novelist, best known for *The Living End.*

EMERSON, RALPH WALDO (1803–1882) American poet, essayist, and leading Transcendentalist thinker, who preached the value of self-reliance and of instinct over reason.

EMPEDOCLES (c. 490–430 B.C.) Greek philosopher, statesman, poet, and religious teacher.

EPICTETUS (55–c. 135) Phrygian Stoic philosopher, known for his emphasis on the inner self rather than worldly objects.

EURIPIDES (c. 484–406 B.C.) Greek dramatist known for the tragedies *Medea, Orestes, Electra,* and *Trojan Women.*

EVAGRIUS OF PONTUS (346–399) Christian mystic and noted preacher in Constantinople; after a spiritual crisis he withdrew to the Egyptian desert where he evolved his mystical theology.

FADIMAN, CLIFTON (1904–1999) Writer, editor at *The New Yorker,* probably best known as the knowledgeable host of the radio show *Information Please.*

FENTON, JAMES (1949–) English poet, journalist, and professor at Oxford.

FOSDICK, HARRY EMERSON (1878–1969) American liberal Protestant minister, author of *A Faith for Tough Times.*

FREUD, SIGMUND (1856–1939) Austrian "father of psychology" who pioneered theories of the unconscious and developed the technique called psychoanalysis.

FULLER, BUCKMINSTER (1895–1983) American philosopher, visionary, poet, cosmologist, engineer, and inventor of the geodesic dome. One of the first futurists, he wrote *Operating Manual for Spaceship Earth.*

GAIMAN, NEIL (1960–) and PRATCHETT, TERRY (1948–) English fantasy and horror authors who collaborated on the novel *Good Omens.*

GANDHI, MOHANDAS (1869–1948) Indian political and spiritual leader, the "Father of India" whose practice of non-violent action (*satyagraha*) threw off the yoke of British rule.

GIBRAN, KAHLIL (1883–1931) Lebanese-American writer whose work *The Prophet* is known worldwide.

GIDE, ANDRÉ (1869–1951) Prolific French writer, humanist, moralist, and outspoken champion of the poor.

GILMAN, CHARLOTTE PERKINS (1860–1935) American feminist and writer, whose works were rediscovered in the 1970s.

GOETHE, JOHANN WOLFGANG VON (1749–1832) German novelist, playwright, philosopher, poet, and polymath; author of *Faust.*

GOGH, VINCENT VAN (1853–1890) Dutch painter of *Starry Night* and other masterpieces. His inwardly rich but impoverished life, punctuated by episodes of madness, was eloquently revealed in his letters to his brother, Theo.

GOULD, STEPHEN JAY (1941–2002) American paleontologist and evolutionary biologist, author of *The Mismeasure of Man.*

GREENE, GRAHAM (1904–1991) English author known for his exotic travels, his conversion to Catholicism, and novels such as *The Power and the Glory* and *The End of the Affair*.

GUITRY, SACHA (1885–1957) French actor, film director, and dramatist who wrote *Nono* and *Le Veilleur de nuit*.

GUNTHER, JOHN (1901–1970) American journalist and author of the memoir *Death Be Not Proud*.

HAFIZ (c. 1325–1389) Persian lyric poet famous for the *Divan*. At the age of 60, longing to be united with his Creator, he began a 40-day and -night vigil by sitting within a circle.

HALEVI, JUDAH (c. 1075–1141) Spanish Jewish poet and philosopher.

HAMMARSKJÖLD, DAG (1905–1961) Swedish statesman, secretary-general of the United Nations, posthumous winner of the Nobel Peace Prize, and author of *Markings*.

HAWKING, STEPHEN WILLIAM (1942–) British physicist who elucidated cosmology and black holes in his work *A Brief History of Time*.

HEINE, HEINRICH (1797–1856) Preeminent German lyrical poet, known for *Buch der Lieder* (*The Book of Songs*).

HEMINGWAY, ERNEST (1899–1961) American expatriate writer, winner of the Nobel Prize, creator of a terse, staccato style and modern hero who defined courage as "grace under pressure."

HERACLITUS (c. 540–c. 480 B.C.) Greek philosopher; known in later life as the "weeping philosopher."

HERBERT, GEORGE (1593–1633) English metaphysical poet and Anglican priest who wrote of the "spiritual conflicts that have passed betwixt God and my soul."

HESCHEL, RABBI ABRAHAM JOSHUA (1907–1972) American theologian, philosopher, and social activist, whose best-known work is *God in Search of Man: A Philosophy of Judaism.*

HÖLDERLIN, FRIEDRICH (1770–1843) German classical-romantic poet known for his lyrical verses.

HOPKINS, GERARD MANLEY (1844–1889) English Jesuit priest whose poetry often explored his relationship to God—from spiritual struggle to ecstatic vision.

HUXLEY, SIR JULIAN (1887–1975) English biologist and writer.

INGE, WILLIAM RALPH (1860–1954) English academic, writer, and theologian at Oxford and Cambridge and Dean of St. Paul's Cathedral, London.

IRENAEUS, SAINT (c. 125–c. 202) Greek theologian, Bishop of Lyon, whose *Against Heresies* was a refutation of Gnosticism.

JACKSON, MAHALIA (1911–1972) American gospel singer ("The Queen of Gospel Song") and civil rights activist, known for her powerful, joyful performances.

JAMES, WILLIAM (1842–1910) Brilliant, original American philosopher and psychologist known for his work *The Varieties of Religious Experience.*

JARMAN, MARK (1952–) American essayist and poet whose collections include *Questions for Ecclesiastes: Poems.*

JOHNSON, SAMUEL (1709–1784) English writer, scholar, and lexicographer, known to us through Boswell's *Life of Johnson.*

JOYCE, JAMES (1882–1941) Irish novelist, poet, expatriate, lapsed Catholic; author of *Ulysses* and *Portrait of an Artist as a Young Man.*

JULIAN OF NORWICH, DAME (1342–c.1416) English anchoress, mystic, and author of *Revelations of Divine Love.*

JUNG, CARL GUSTAV (1875–1961) Swiss psychiatrist who broke with Freud and founded analytic psychology. Known for his theories of archetypes and the collective unconscious.

KABIR (1440–1518) Indian mystic and popular poet, some of whose work was incorporated into the sacred book of the Sikhs, *Adi Granth.*

KAFKA, FRANZ (1883–1924) Czech novelist who wrote in German about alienation, guilt, and anxiety, and whose works include *Metamorphosis* and *The Trial.*

KAZANTZAKIS, NIKOS (1885–1957) Greek poet, philosopher, and author of *The Last Temptation of Chist, Zorba the Greek,* and *The Odyssey: A Modern Sequel.*

KELLER, HELEN (1880–1968) American author, lecturer, and writer. Blind and deaf from an early age, she was taught by Anne Sullivan and eventually graduated from Radcliffe with honors. Works include *The Story of My Life* and *My Religion.*

KEROUAC, JACK (1922–1969) American novelist, poet, and founder of the Beat Generation, author of *On the Road* and *Dharma Bums.*

KIERKEGAARD, SØREN (1813–1855) Danish religious philosopher and author of *Either/Or* and *Fear and Trembling.*

KOESTLER, ARTHUR (1905–1983) Hungarian-born British novelist, social philosopher, and political activist. Author of *Darkness at Noon* and *The God that Failed.*

KOTZK, RABBI MENACHEM MENDEL OF (1787–1859) A Polish leader of the Hasidic movement.

KRISHNAMURTI, JIDDU (1895–1986) Charismatic Indian spiritual teacher, embraced by the Theosophists, but later an independent guru based in California. Books include *Freedom from the Known* and *Awakening of Intelligence.*

LAING, R. D. (1927–1989) British psychiatrist noted for his alternative approach to the treatment of schizophrenia, and author of *The Divided Self.*

LAMOTT, ANNE (1954–) Contemporary American author of *Traveling Mercies, Operating Instructions,* and the classic work on writing and life, *Bird by Bird.*

LASKER-SCHULER, ELSE (1869–1945) Early German expressionist poet, playwright, and novelist. After her work was banned by the Nazis, she fled to Switzerland and later to Jerusalem, where she died.

LAWRENCE, D. H. (1885–1930) English novelist, poet, and critic whose works include *Sons and Lovers, The Rainbow,* and *Women in Love.*

LEE, MOTHER ANN (1736–1784) Founder of the first American Shaker colony.

LENNON, JOHN (1940–1980) English songwriter and founding member of the Beatles, celebrated for his music, integrity, political activism, and peace initiatives, perhaps best articulated in the song "Imagine."

LENYA, LOTTE (1900–1981) Austrian singer, character actress, and wife of the composer Kurt Weill. Perhaps best remembered for her portrayal of both Jenny and Lucy in *The Threepenny Opera.*

LERNER, MAX (1902–1992) American writer, teacher, columnist, and liberal political advocate.

LEWIS, C. S. (1898–1963) English author of *Mere Christianity* and *Screwtape Letters,* as well as fantasy novels.

LINCOLN, ABRAHAM (1809–1865) The 16th and perhaps most eloquent American president, credited with ending slavery and preserving the Union through the Civil War.

LOGAU, FRIEDRICH VON (1604–1655) German epigrammist whose works include *First Hundred German Proverbs in Rhyme.*

MACLEISH, ARCHIBALD (1892–1982) American poet who was also an undersecretary of state. His works include *New Found Land* and the verse drama *J.B.,* based on the life of Job.

MAIMONIDES, MOSES (1135–1204) Spanish physician, philosopher, and leading Jewish scholar who organized oral Jewish law into Mishneh Torah.

MANDELSTAM, OSIP (1891–1938) Russian poet and essayist. Arrested for writing an epigram about Stalin in 1934, he was arrested again in 1938 for counterrevolutionary activity and died soon after in the Gulag Archipelago.

McCOURT, FRANK (1931–) American-Irish novelist and teacher; won the Pulitzer Prize for *Angela's Ashes.*

MECHTILD OF MAGDEBURG (1207–1282) German visionary and poet whose work, such as *The Flowing Light of the Godhead,* is said to have inspired Dante.

MELVILLE, HERMAN (1819–1891) American author of *Moby Dick,* among other classics; first went to sea as a cabin boy in 1839.

MENCKEN, H. L. (1880–1956) American writer, co-founder of *American Mercury,* and acerbic critic of the middle class; his writings are collected in the six-volume *Prejudices.*

MERTON, THOMAS (1915–68) American Catholic writer, poet, Trappist monk, and author of *The Seven Storey Mountain,* which records his spiritual odyssey.

MILLAY, EDNA ST. VINCENT (1892–1950) American poet, preeminent member of the bohemian group that flourished in Greenwich Village in the 1920s, and winner of the Pulitzer Prize for *Ballad of the Harp-Weaver.*

MILLER, HENRY (1891–1980) Spirited, iconoclastic American author, notably of the *Tropic of Cancer*.

MIRABAI (c. 1498–1547) Hindu mystic and the most famous of the female *bhakta* (love) poets of north India.

MITFORD, NANCY (1904–1973) English satirical novelist and one of six famed Mitford sisters; author of the highly autobiographical *Pursuit of Love* and *Love in a Cold Climate*.

MONTAIGNE, MICHEL DE (1533–1592) French Renaissance essayist who undertook the study of mankind by studying himself.

MONTESQUIEU, CHARLES, BARON DE (1689–1755) French political philosopher and author of *The Spirit of Laws*.

MORLEY, CHRISTOPHER (1890–1957) American author and one of the founding editors of *Saturday Review of Literature*.

MUKTABAI (13th century) Indian author of legendary religious and philosophical verse; little else is known of her.

MUHAMMAD (c. 570–632) Arab prophet, founder of Islam, "author" of the Qur'an, which is traditionally considered to have been dictated to him by the angel Gabriel.

MURRAY, PAUL (1947–) Dominican priest, poet, and lecturer on mystical theology.

NATHAN, GEORGE JEAN (1882–1958) American editor, drama critic, and co-founder of *American Mercury.*

NIETZSCHE, FRIEDRICH (1844–1900) German philosopher who rejected conventional morality and conceived of the "superman" who was above simple standards of good and evil; author of *Thus Spake Zarathustra* and *Beyond Good and Evil.*

NORGAY, TENZIG (1914–1986) Sherpa mountaineer and devout Buddhist, won fame in 1953 when he and Sir Edmund Hillary became the first to scale Mt. Everest. The story of the climb is related in his autobiography, *Man of Everest.*

NOUWEN, HENRI J. M. (1932–1996) Dutch Catholic priest, theologian, and author of works on prayer and the spiritual life.

O'NEILL, EUGENE (1888–1953) Nobel Prize–winning American dramatist, author of 50 plays, including *The Iceman Cometh* and *Long Day's Journey into Night.*

OLIVIER, SIR LAURENCE (1907–1989) Celebrated English actor and director who won an Academy Award for his Hamlet, but was equally at home playing a villainous retired Nazi in *Marathon Man*.

OSBORNE, JOAN (1963–) American singer-songwriter whose spiritually themed lyrics appear on such albums as *Soul Show* and *Righteous Love*.

PASCAL, BLAISE (1623–1662) French mathematician, scientist, and philosopher known for his *Pensées*.

PASTEUR, LOUIS (1822–1895) French chemist famous for work on minimizing bacteria that led to the process of pasteurization.

PHILO (c. 15 B.C.–c. A.D. 45) Alexandrian Jewish philosopher whose writings have had an enormous influence on Judeo-Christian thought.

PICASSO, PABLO (1881–1973) Prolific Spanish painter (*Guernica, Three Musicians*), sculptor, pioneer of Cubism; famed for artistic innovation and versatility.

PILLAR, KENNETH (1924–) Suffragan Bishop of Hertford, in the diocese of St. Albans, England.

PLATH, SYLVIA (1932–1963) American poet known for her acutely personal and sometimes shocking writing and for her autobiography *The Bell Jar.*

POTOK, CHAIM (1929–2002) Conservative rabbi and author of such novels as *The Chosen* and *My Name Is Asher Lev.*

RABI'A (717–801) A Sufi mystic poet and Muslim saint.

RAMAKRISHNA (1836–1886) Hindu mystic and saint who held the view that all religions are a valid means for finding God. His teachings are preserved in *The Gospel of Ramakrishna.*

RAVITCH, MELECH (1893–1976) Yiddish poet and essayist whose collections include *Night Prayer and Other Poems.*

RENARD, JULES (1864–1910) French novelist and playwright, best known for his autographical *Poil de carette.*

RICHTER, JEAN PAUL (1763–1825) Popular German author of *The Invisible Lodge* and *Hesperus.*

RILKE, RAINER MARIA (1875–1926) Widely translated Austro-German poet known for his *Sonnets to Orpheus, Duino Elegies,* and *Letters to a Young Poet.*

ROIPHE, ANNE (1935–) American feminist writer and columnist whose best-known novel is *Up the Sandbox!*

ROTHMAN, LILY (1986–) New York high school student.

RUMI, JALAL AD-DIN (1207–1273) Persian poet and founder of the Mawlawiyah Sufi order. His six-volume epic work, the *Mathnawi*, concerns itself, as does much of his poetry, with the absolute love of God.

RUSKIN, JOHN (1819–1900) English art critic and social theorist; author of *Stones of Venice*.

RUSSELL, BERTRAND (1872–1970) British philosopher, famed for the landmark work on logic and mathematics, *The Principia Mathematica*.

RUYSBROECK, JAN VAN (1293–1381) Flemish mystic whose *Spiritual Espousals* discusses his view of the Trinity.

SA'ID, ABU (967–1049) Sufi mystic, credited with establishing rules of Sufi conduct. His love poems to God have been translated in *Nobody, Son of Nobody*.

SALZMAN, MARK (1959–) Contemporary American writer, author of *Iron and Silk* and *Lying Awake,* about a Carmelite nun visited by ecstatic visions of God's radiance.

SAND, GEORGE (Pseudonym of Aurore Dudevant) (1804–1876) Influential 19th-century French woman writer, equally well known for her prolific writings and for her colorful personal life.

SANDBURG, CARL (1878–1967) American poet and journalist known for his plain-spoken language, themes of American history, and belief in the common man.

SARTRE, JEAN-PAUL (1905–1980) French philosopher, playwright, existentialist, author of *No Exit* and *Being and Nothingness.*

SASAKI ROSHI, JOSSHU (1907–) Zen master who came to America and established centers around his rigorous Rinzai practice, which stresses the abrupt awakening of enlightenment.

SENECA (4 B.C./A.D. 1–A.D. 65) Roman philosopher, orator, diplomat, statesman, and poet whose writings discuss practical ethics modeled on the philosophy of Stoicism.

SERVICE, ROBERT (1874–1958) English-born Canadian poet whose popular songs, rhymes, and ballads capture the spirit of wanderlust.

SEXTON, ANNE (1928–1974) American "confessional" poet who won the Pulitzer Prize for the collection *Live or Die. He*r painful *The Awful Rowing Toward God* was published after her suicide.

SHAKESPEARE, WILLIAM (1564–1616) English playwright and poet widely acknowledged as the writer who held up a mirror to mankind.

SHEED, WILFRID (1930–) Contemporary American novelist and essayist.

SHELLEY, PERCY BYSSHE (1792–1822) English romantic poet with radical political, social, and philosophical ideas who was notorious for his unorthodox lifestyle.

SILESIUS, ANGELUS (1624–1677) German priest, monastic, and poet, most famous for *The Cherubic Wanderer.*

SINGER, ISAAC BASHEVIS (1904–91) American novelist and short-story writer who, working in Yiddish, explored themes from Jewish folklore and mysticism and who won a Nobel Prize for Literature.

SITWELL, DAME EDITH (1887–1964) Eccentric English poet and writer. During World War II she began to write religious poetry and she converted to Catholicism in 1954.

SMART, CHRISTOPHER (1722–1771) English poet and brilliant classical scholar who was overtaken by religious mania and committed to St. Luke's Hospital in 1756. *Song to David,* his best-known work, was written during this time.

SPINOZA, BARUCH (BENEDICT) (1632–1677) Dutch philosopher whose works such as *A Treatise on Religious and Political Philosophy* were considered blasphemous and not published in his lifetime.

STEVENS, WALLACE (1879–1955) American poet who believed in the regenerative and redemptive act of imagining and reimagining. He won a Pulitzer Prize for *Collected Poems* in 1954.

STOPPARD, TOM (1937–) English playwright most recognized for his Hamlet parody, *Rosencrantz and Guildenstern Are Dead.*

SWINBURNE, ALGERNON CHARLES (1837–1909) English poet and critic who won fame for the play *Atalanta in Calydon.*

SZASZ, THOMAS (1920–) Hungarian-American psychiatrist who rebelled against his profession in his work *The Myth of Mental Illness.*

TAGORE, SIR RABINDRANATH (1861–1941) Indian author, poet, guru, critic of violence and the Indian caste system.

TAULER, JOHANNES (c. 1300–1361) German mystic considered one of the greatest medieval preachers.

TENNYSON, ALFRED LORD (1809–1892) English poet who suffered from melancholy throughout his life; found fame after publishing *In Memoriam,* a work which took 17 years to complete and reflects his lifelong conflict between faith and doubt.

TERESA, MOTHER (1910–1997) Roman Catholic missionary in India who won the 1979 Nobel Peace Prize. Her best-known work is *No Greater Love.*

THOMAS, DYLAN (1914–1953) Welsh poet whose work of burning intensity "is the record of my individual struggle from darkness toward some measure of light."

THOMAS, R. S. (1913–) Welsh poet, ordained by the Anglican church, published *Stones of the Field* and *The Bread of Truth*.

TILLICH, PAUL (1886–1965) German-born American philosopher and theologian whose best-known works are *Systematic Theology* and *The Courage to Be*.

TOLSTOY, LEO (1828–1910) Russian writer and moralist; pioneer of the "psychological novel." His *War and Peace* and *Anna Karenina* are considered two of the world's preeminent novels.

TUKARAM (1608–1649) Indian poet and itinerant ascetic, penned over 4,000 hymns.

TWAIN, MARK (pseudonym of Samuel Langhorne Clemens) (1835–1910) American author of *Tom Sawyer, The Adventures of Huckleberry Finn,* and many other works. Twain's opinions about man and religion soured deeply over the years.

UNAMUNO, MIGUEL DE (1864–1936) Spanish philosopher, novelist, and early existentialist who explored the tension between faith and reason in *The Agony of Christianity.*

UPDIKE, JOHN (1932–) Contemporary American novelist, poet, and critic. His many novels include *Roger's Version,* which revolves around a discussion of scientifically proving the existence of God.

VAUGHAN, HENRY (1622–1695) British poet who studied both law and medicine. His third collection of poetry, *Silex Scintillans,* sought "shadows of eternity" in natural phenomena.

VOLTAIRE (FRANÇOIS MARIE AROUET DE) (1694–1778) French philosopher, writer, and satirist; principal champion of European Enlightenment.

WATTS, ISAAC (1674–1748) English clergyman, poet, and hymn writer whose *Psalms of David* contains some of the most famous hymns in English.

WEBSTER, DANIEL (1782–1852) American lawyer, statesman, and orator.

WEIL, SIMONE (1909–1943) French philosopher, raised in an agnostic Jewish family, converted to Catholicism and wrote deeply about God, religion, and mysticism. Her works, published posthumously, include *Gravity and Grace* and *Waiting for God.*

WHITEHEAD, ALFRED NORTH (1861–1947) English mathematician and philosopher, best known for *Science and the Modern World,* which outlines his mathematically based belief in God the Absolute.

WHITMAN, WALT (1819–1892) American poet whose *Leaves of Grass* profoundly influenced modern poetry and American culture.

WIESEL, ELIE (1928–) Romanian-born American writer; imprisoned in Nazi concentration camps at 16; won Nobel Peace Prize for his efforts to help oppressed people, author of 36 works focusing on the Holocaust, including the memoir *Night.*

WILLIAMS, TENNESSEE (1911–1983) American dramatist who won Pulitzer prizes for *A Streetcar Named Desire* and *Cat on a Hot Tin Roof.*

WOOLF, VIRGINIA (1882–1941) English writer and member of the Bloomsbury group. She helped pioneer stream-of-consciousness writing in works such as *Mrs. Dalloway* and *To the Lighthouse*.

WRIGHT, FRANK LLOYD (1869–1959) Pioneering American architect known for his organic style; noted for such buildings as Fallingwater, Unity Temple, and the Guggenheim Museum. Author of *An Autobiography* and *An Organic Architecture*.

WRIGHT, JAMES (1927–1980) American poet who early in his career was preoccupied with themes of guilt and suffering. Collections include *The Green Wall* and *Saint Judas*.

YOSEF OF POLNOYE, RABBI YAAKOV (c. 1669–1781) The foremost disciple of Baal Shem Tov, author of the first book on Hasidic philosophy.

XENOPHANES (c. 560–c. 478 B.C.) Greek poet, philosopher, and founder of Eleatic philosophy, which stressed unity over diversity.

ZANGWILL, ISRAEL (1864–1926) English novelist, playwright, and prominent Zionist whose works include *Children of the Ghetto* and the play *The Melting Pot*.

We gratefully acknowledge the following for permission to reprint material copyrighted or controlled by them. Every effort has been made to clear reprints. If any required credits have been omitted or any rights overlooked, it is unintentional, and we will gladly correct any omissions in future reprints.